D1474524

REASONS TO CARE ABOUT
RHINOS
[Animals in Peril]

Mary Firestone

Enslow Publishers, Inc.
40 Industrial Road
Box 398
Berkeley Heights, NJ 07922
USA
http://www.enslow.com

Library of Congress Cataloguing-in-Publication Data
Firestone, Mary.
  Top 50 reasons to care about rhinos : animals in peril / by Mary Firestone.
      p. cm. – (Top 50 reasons to care about endangered animals)
  Includes bibliographical references and index.
  Summary: "Readers will learn about the different types of rhino, their life cycle, diet, young, habitat, and reasons why they are endangered animals"–Provided by publisher.
  ISBN 978-0-7660-3457-0
  1. Rhinoceroses–Juvenile literature. 2. Endangered species–Juvenile literature. I. Title. II. Title: Top fifty reasons to care about rhinos.
  QL737.U63F57 2010
  599.66'8–dc22
                              2008048692

Printed in the United States of America

092009 Lake Book Manufacturing, Inc., Melrose Park, IL

10 9 8 7 6 5 4 3 2 1

Enslow Publishers, Inc., is committed to printing our books on recycled paper. The paper in every book contains 10% and 30% post-consumer waste (PCW). The cover board on the outside of each book contains 100% PCW. Our goal is to do our part to help young people and the environment too!

Photographs: Jan Rysavy/iStockphoto, cover inset, 1; Michael Price/iStockphoto, 1; Ingo Arndt/Nature Picture Library, 4; Red Line Editorial, 6; Peter Blackwell/Nature Picture Library, 9; Wegner/ARCO/Nature Picture Library, 10; Shiran De Silva/iStockphoto, 13; Hilton Kotze/iStockphoto, 14, 28; Graeme Purdy/iStockphoto, 17; Anup Shah/Nature Picture Library, 18, 26 (top); Jordao Henrique/AP Images, 20; David Tipling/Nature Picture Library, 21; Richard Du Toit/Nature Picture Library, 22, 34; Jeremy Richards/iStockphoto, 23; iStockphoto, 25, 67; Mark Kostich/iStockphoto, 26 (bottom); Pauline Mills/iStockphoto, 29; Matt Ellis/iStockphoto, 30; Kitch Bain/iStockphoto, 31; Sharon Heald/Nature Picture Library, 33, 48; Stephen Meese/iStockphoto, 35; Wolfgang Steiner/iStockphoto, 36; Nico Smit/iStockphoto, 38, 99; George Cairns/iStockphoto, 41; Tony Heald/Nature Picture Library, 42; Joseph White/iStockphoto, 43; Henri Faure/iStockphoto, 44; Pete Oxford/Nature Picture Library, 45; Michael Hutchinson/Nature Picture Library, 47; Mark Weiss/iStockphoto, 50; Stephen Earle/iStockphoto, 51; T.J. Rich/Nature Picture Library, 53; Lisa Asch/Nature Picture Library, 54; Alejandro Sanz Torrente/iStockphoto, 56; Alain Couillaud/iStockphoto, 59; Steven L. Raymer/National Geographic/Getty Images, 60; Tom Uhlman/AP Images, 63; Vivek Menon/Nature Picture Library, 64; Nick Upton/Nature Picture Library, 68; Mark Carwardine/Nature Picture Library, 71; AP Images, 72; Nigel Tucker/Nature Picture Library, 75; Rick Olson/iStockphoto, 76; John Downer/Nature Picture Library, 78; David Freund/iStockphoto, 81; Hemanta Kumar Nat/AP Images, 82; Chris Howland/iStockphoto, 84; Mark Payne-Gill/Nature Picture Library, 85; Dawn Nichols/iStockphoto, 86; Bernard Castelein/Nature Picture Library, 89; Bruce Davidson/Nature Picture Library, 90, 94; Nature Production/Nature Picture Library, 93; Rod Williams/Nature Picture Library, 97

Cover caption: A white rhinoceros mother protects her calf.
Michael Price/iStockphoto

CONTENTS

ENDANGERED RHINOCEROSES

Thousands of years ago, millions of rhinoceroses roamed the continents of Asia and Africa. Around one hundred and fifty years ago, millions of rhinos still remained on the African plains and in the rain forests of Asia.

In 2008, there were only about twenty-five thousand rhinos still alive on Earth. Nearly all of them live in protected areas, which are monitored by law enforcement officers.

The trouble for rhinos began around one hundred years ago when Europeans on hunting expeditions killed them by the thousands. Today, it is illegal to hunt a rhino. Poachers still kill rhinos for their horns, which are sold on the black market.

Loss of habitat also threatens rhinos. As human populations spread out from cities, trees are cut down and houses are built over prairies. Without their habitat, rhinos cannot find food.

Conservation groups are tackling these threats. Their work is critical to the survival of rhinos. Without it, rhinos might have become extinct already. However, conservation efforts need everyone's help. We all can make a difference in the survival of the rhino species.

◀ THE RHINOCEROS IS THREATENED WITH EXTINCTION.

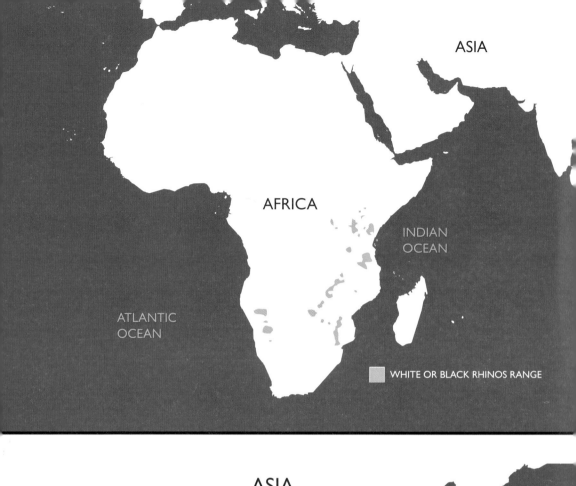

ASIA

AFRICA

INDIAN
OCEAN

ATLANTIC
OCEAN

■ WHITE OR BLACK RHINOS RANGE

ASIA

INDIAN
OCEAN

PACIFIC
OCEAN

■ SUMATRAN RHINOS RANGE

■ INDIAN RHINOS RANGE

□ JAVAN RHINOS RANGE

GETTING TO KNOW RHINOS

REASON TO CARE # 1
Rhinos Are Unique

There is no mistaking the rhinoceros. With its enormous body, stubby legs, and long, pointed horn, it is unique among the world's mammals.

Until 5 million years ago, the rhinoceros was one of the most common large mammals on the continents of Africa, Asia, Europe, and North America. Today, only five species remain in Asia and Africa, and these species are all in danger of becoming extinct.

[The name rhinoceros comes from the Greek language. It means "horned-nose."]

◄ TOP: TWO SPECIES OF RHINOS LIVE IN AFRICA. BOTTOM: THREE SPECIES OF RHINOS LIVE IN ASIA.

Rhinos Are Prehistoric

Rhinos have lived on Earth for more than 50 million years, roaming the continents of North America, Europe, Africa, and Asia. Remains of prehistoric rhino species show that they came in many shapes and sizes. Some rhino species resembled horses; others looked like hippos. One small rhino was less than 3 feet (1 meter) tall.

Prehistoric rhinos were not limited to tropical zones like the rhinos of today. They also lived in temperate climates and even in areas near the Arctic. Prehistoric humans drew scenes in caves of the woolly rhino being hunted. Woolly rhinos lived in Europe and Asia until about ten thousand years ago, but they are now extinct.

▶ ANCIENT ROCK ART FROM NAMIBIA FEATURING A RHINOCEROS

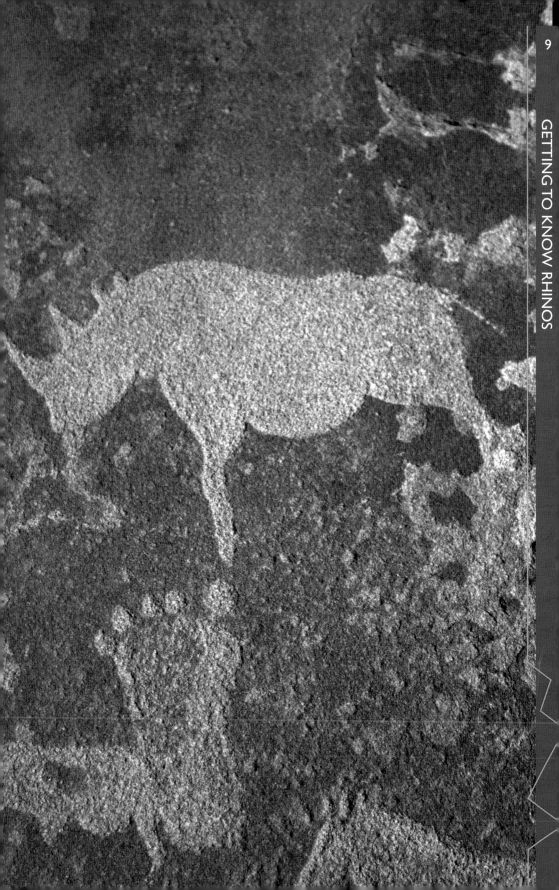

REASON TO CARE # 3
Rhinos Have Species and Subspecies

Rhinos belong to an order of mammals known as Perissodactyls. Horses, donkeys, and zebras are also members of this group. A Perissodactyl is an animal that eats plants and has an odd number of hoofed toes.

There are five main rhino species in existence today: the African white rhino, the African black rhino, and the three Asian rhino species, which are the Indian, the Sumatran, and the Javan.

There are four subspecies of the black rhino and two subspecies of the white rhino. Some of these subspecies exist in tiny numbers, as small as five or six. The West African black rhino, a black rhino subspecies, is thought to be completely extinct.

[Rhinos usually live about thirty-five years. Some rhinos can live as long as fifty years.]

◀ RHINOCEROSES HAVE HOOFED TOES. SOME SPECIES OF RHINOS HAVE MORE TOES THAN OTHERS.

Rhinos Live in Africa and Asia

The two species of African rhinos, the black rhino and the white rhino, live in populations scattered across Eastern, Central, Western, and Southern Africa. They live on savannas, on tropical grasslands, and in forests.

Asian rhinos live in the tropical areas of India and Southeast Asia. They prefer forests, marshes, and grassy areas next to rivers. In Asia, Javan rhinos live deep within the rain forests, where they can find all the swamps, trees, and leaves they need. Indian rhinos live mainly near rivers in the foothills of the Himalayan Mountains. Sumatran rhinos live in tropical cloud forests in the mountains.

[Cloud forests are a type of rain forest that occurs at high altitudes in tropical areas around the world. They are usually blanketed in clouds and mist.]

▶ MANY AFRICAN RHINOCEROSES LIVE ON SAVANNAS.

REASON TO CARE # 5

Black Rhinos
Are Not Black

The African black rhino is not really black. Its skin is actually gray. It also has a pointed, prehensile upper lip, which allows it to easily grip with its mouth. Some call the black rhino the hook-lipped rhino. Black rhinos weigh about 1,750 to 3,000 pounds (800 to 1,400 kilograms), have two horns, and stand 5 feet (1.5 meters) tall at the shoulder.

Black rhinos usually live alone, except when it is time to mate. Then, males and females come together for a few days. Black rhino mothers and calves travel together, but as the calf matures, they split apart and travel alone.

[The black rhino's scientific name is *Diceros bicornis*. *Bicornis* means "two horns."]

◄ BLACK RHINOCEROSES HAVE A POINTED, PREHENSILE LIP.

White Rhinos Are Not White

White rhinos have gray skin and a wide, flat upper lip. Some say the white rhino became known as such because its skin is a little lighter than the black rhino's. Others say Europeans called them "wide-mouthed" rhinos, which later became shortened and mistakenly changed to "white."

The white rhino and the Indian rhino are the largest rhinoceroses. Adult male white rhinos weigh around 5,500 pounds (2,500 kilograms) and stand 6 feet (2 meters) tall at the shoulder. White rhinos, like black rhinos, have two horns, which can grow up to 6 feet long.

Unlike solitary black rhinos, white rhinos live in family groups.

[The white rhino's scientific name is *Ceratotherium simum*. There are two white rhino subspecies: northern white rhinos and southern white rhinos.]

▶ WHITE RHINOCEROSES HAVE A FLAT UPPER LIP.

REASON TO CARE # 7

Indian Rhinos Have Brown Skin

The Indian rhino is also known as the one-horned rhino. It has thick, brownish skin that folds at the shoulders, hips, and rump. The skin hangs in a long flap near the rhino's belly and near the top of its front legs. These folds and the skin's knobby surface make the Indian rhino look like it is wearing armor. Adult male Indian rhinos usually weigh about 5,000 pounds (2,300 kilograms) and stand 6 feet (2 meters) at the shoulder.

The Indian rhino's single horn grows to about 20 inches long. All Asian rhinos—the Indian, the Javan, and the Sumatran—have a pointed, prehensile upper lip.

[The Indian rhino's scientific name is *Rhinoceros unicornis*. *Unicornis* means "one horn."]

◄ INDIAN RHINOCEROSES ONLY HAVE ONE HORN.

Javan Rhinos Have Thick, Folded Skin

The Javan rhino has a fold of skin across its neck and shoulders, and another fold at the base of its tail. An average adult male weighs around 2,500 pounds (1,100 kilograms), and stands 5 feet (1.5 meters) tall, about the same size as the black rhino. A Javan rhino's skin has a textured appearance and its single horn is smaller than the Indian rhino's. Females have a small horn, or no horn at all. Its scientific name is *Rhinoceros sondaicus*.

▼ SOME FEMALE JAVAN RHINOCEROSES HAVE NO HORNS.

▲ THE SUMATRAN RHINOCEROS IS THE ONLY LIVING RHINO WITH BODY HAIR.

REASON TO CARE # 9

Sumatran Rhinos Are the Smallest Rhinos

The Sumatran rhino is the only Asian rhino that has two horns. It is also the smallest of all the world's rhinos. It stands only 4 feet (1.2 meters) tall at the shoulder and weighs around 1,500 pounds (700 kilograms). The Sumatran rhino has brownish skin and reddish-brown hair all over its body. Some Sumatran rhinos have longer patches of hair on their back, face, and ears.

[Other names for Sumatran rhinos are hairy rhinoceros and Asian two-horned rhinoceros. Its scientific name is *Dicerorhinus sumatrensis.*]

REASON TO CARE # 10
Only Five Species of Rhinos Remain

The many types of rhinos from the past have been vastly reduced. Today, only three species of rhinos live in Asia: the Sumatran, the Indian, and the Javan. Most of these animals live in protected environments because of the threat of extinction. There are fewer than three thousand rhinos left in Asia.

▼ WHITE RHINOCEROS

▲ INDIAN RHINOCEROS

One African species, the white rhino, is faring better, with more than seventeen thousand rhinos surviving in the wild. The other African species, the black rhino, is nearly extinct. Fewer than four thousand black rhinos remain in the wild. Most rhinos in Africa also live in protected areas, which are usually monitored by law enforcement officers to capture poachers.

[According to the International Rhino Foundation, the Sumatran rhino is the most endangered of all rhinos because its already low numbers are declining rapidly and its habitat is very restricted.]

Rhinos Help
Their Habitats Thrive

Conservationists have designated rhinos a flagship species for their habitats. A flagship species draws attention to and support for the needs of the environment it lives in. Flagship species, such as rhinos and elephants, need a lot of area to move around if they are going to survive. If the focus remains on them and they are protected, then their habitats will also survive, helping many other species.

[Other flagship species include: Amur leopards, bearded vultures, black spider monkeys, brown bears, whales, dolphins, clouded leopards, elephants, Eurasian lynx, giant pandas, great apes, humphead wrasses, Iberian lynx, marine turtles, polar bears, saolas, spectacled bears, and tigers.]

▶ SAVING THE RHINOCEROS WILL ALSO HELP PRESERVE OTHER SPECIES IN THEIR HABITATS.

RHINO BIOLOGY

REASON TO CARE # 12

Rhinos Eat a Lot of Food

A rhinoceros is a huge animal. To keep up with its nutritional needs on a diet of only plants, a rhino must spend half of its life eating. A white rhino can eat 50 to 100 pounds of food each day.

[Rhinos push over young trees to get to the leaves and fruit. They press their front feet against the tree until it bends and hold it with their bellies while they eat.]

Rhinos tend to be either browsers or grazers. A browser eats mainly twigs, leaves, and the tender shoots of plants. A grazer, such as the Indian rhino, eats mostly grasses. Indian rhinos also feed on water plants, bamboo shoots, leaves, and shrubs.

[Rhinos drink approximately 15 to 25 gallons of water each day. However, they can go without water for up to five days.]

◀ TOP: THE BLACK RHINO IS A BROWSER. BOTTOM: THE INDIAN RHINO IS A GRAZER.

A Rhino's Horn Grows All Its Life

Rhinoceros horns are different from deer and cattle horns. The rhino's horn grows on its nose instead of the top of its head. It grows throughout the animal's life. The rhino horn is made of keratin, the same substance that forms hair and human fingernails. Other mammals' horns have bone in the center. The keratin forms tightly packed layers. This makes the horns hard enough to punch through a car door!

▼ A RHINO'S HORN IS MADE OF THE SAME MATERIAL AS HAIR AND HUMAN FINGERNAILS.

▲ RHINO HORNS ARE DANGEROUS WEAPONS.

REASON TO CARE # 14

Rhino Horns
Are Good Weapons

The rhino's horn is its main defense. Rhinos charge lions and hyenas who attack their young. Adult rhinos have no predators in the wild because of their size, strength, and horns. Rhinos also use their horns to fight other rhinos. A rhino's horn comes in handy when digging for water and pushing through thick underbrush. African rhinos sharpen their horns by rubbing them on trees and rocks. If a rhino's horn breaks, it will grow back.

Rhinos Cannot See Very Well

If you stood right in front of a rhino, it would not be able to get a good look at you without turning its head. Rhinos' eyes are on the sides of their heads. Rhinos are also nearsighted, which means they cannot see things that are far away. Their horns are another obstacle to vision. Black rhinos sometimes attack large rocks and trees because their eyesight is so poor.

▼ RHINOCEROSES HAVE POOR VISION.

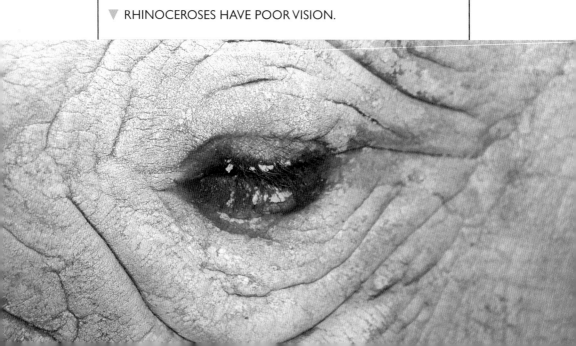

▲ RHINOCEROSES HAVE A STRONG SENSE OF SMELL.

REASON TO CARE # 16

Rhinos Have an Excellent Sense of Smell

Rhinos strongest sense is smell, and they use it to detect danger and know what animals are nearby. If a rhino mother and her calf are ever separated, they can find each other by sniffing the other's trail in the grass or soil. Rhinos mark their territory with dung heaps and sprays of urine. Other rhinos can sense these markers and know to stay away. Female rhinos spray urine to let males know they are ready to mate.

Rhinos Use Infrasound

Rhinos communicate in familiar ways: when a baby rhino squeals, its mother comes running. Rhinos grunt and snort when they meet each other. But they also communicate in unusual ways. Adult rhinos rumble with a low frequency sound called infrasound, a noise that is almost impossible for humans to hear. Rhinos use it to communicate with each other over long distances.

[Rhinoceroses make many noises, from squeals and grunts to sounds too deep for humans to hear.]

▶ MALE RHINOS CURL THEIR TAILS WHEN THEY ARE AFRAID OR UPSET. THEY ALSO WILL ROAR DURING A FIGHT.

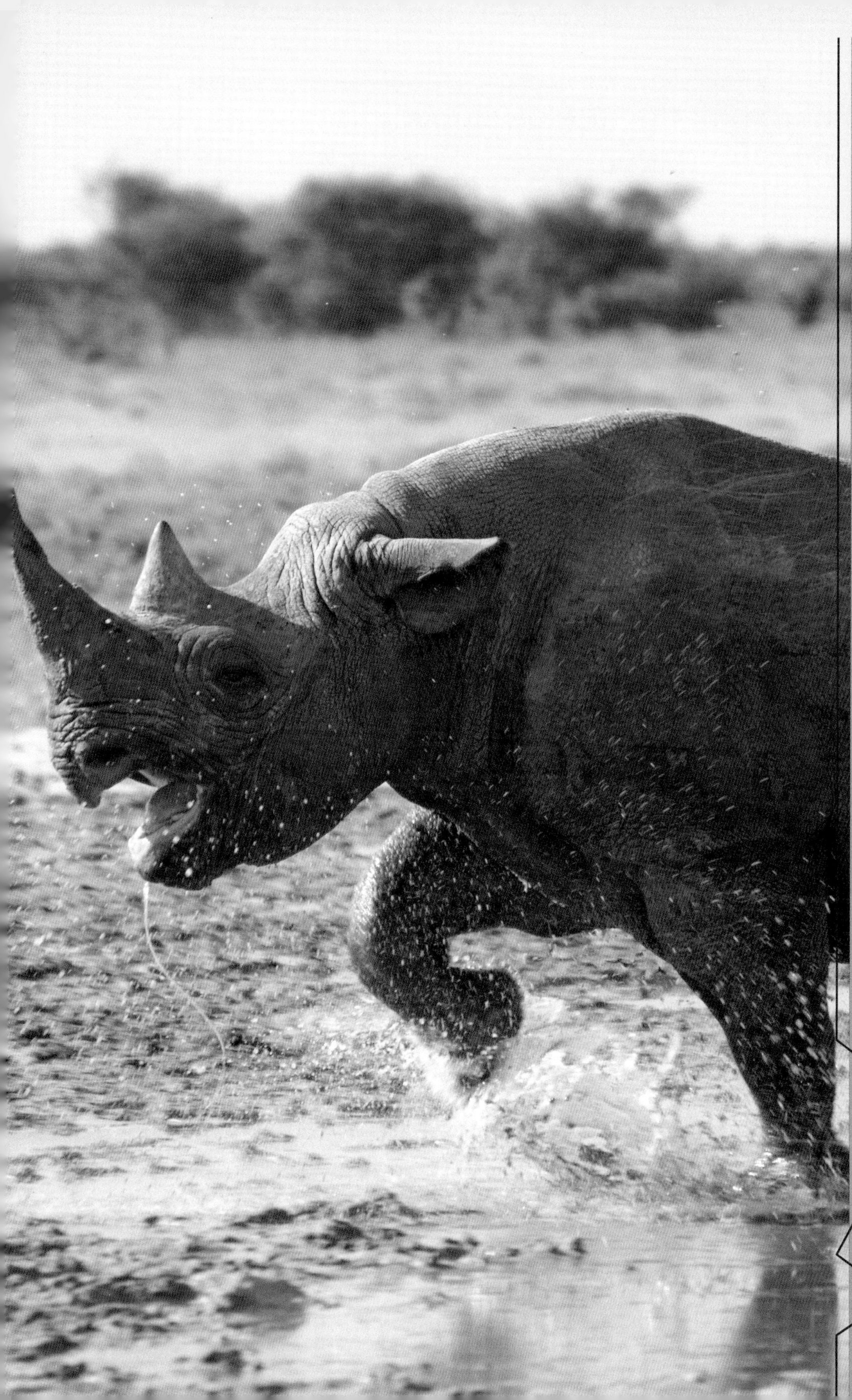

Rhinos Are Always Listening

Rhinos have excellent hearing, which helps make up for their poor eyesight. Rhino ears are always alert, gathering information about the environment. Even when the rhino is asleep, it is listening. Rhino ears are either round or pointed and stand up on each side of the animal's head. They swivel toward the direction of a sound. Then, the rhino uses its sense of smell to assess the situation.

▼ THE EARS OF THIS RHINOCEROS ARE POINTED IN DIFFERENT DIRECTIONS TO PICK UP SOUNDS.

▲ RHINOCEROS EARS CAN SWIVEL TOWARD THE DIRECTION OF SOUNDS.

A rhino cannot see a person standing 100 feet away if that person does not move. However, the rhino's ears will pick up the faintest sound and its sensitive nose tells it when other animals are nearby.

REASON TO CARE # 19

Rhinos Have
No Front Teeth

Rhinos are herbivores, which means they only eat plants and fruit. Their teeth are suited to chewing these foods, which are plentiful in their habitat. For example, white rhinos living on savannas have twelve or fourteen pairs of molars, depending on the subspecies. Molars are blunt teeth in the back of the mouth that are good for grinding up the savanna's tall grasses.

Indian rhinos have molars, but they also have narrow incisors in their lower jaw. These teeth help them grip grasses and pull leaves from branches. The only rhinos with canine teeth (the cone shaped teeth at the sides of the mouth) are Sumatran rhinos.

◄ BLACK AND WHITE RHINOS HAVE NO FRONT TEETH. THEY GRIP GRASSES AND LEAVES WITH THEIR STRONG LIPS.

RHINO BEHAVIOR

REASON TO CARE # 20

Rhinos Stay
on the Savanna

The rainy seasons in the parts of Africa where most rhinos live are in the spring and late fall. During the rest of the year, the savanna is dry. But after it rains, the savanna comes alive with red oat grass, star grass, and guinea grass, creating a feast for rhinos and other herbivores.

During the dry season, rhinos are resourceful about finding water and food. Though the plants and grasses turn brown, they still have plenty of nutrition, and rhinos will eat them.

A lot of the large animals migrate away from the savanna during its dry seasons to other grasslands. Rhinos and elephants stay on the savanna, which is a challenge for elephants because black rhinos are not good at sharing watering holes. Rhinos also dig to reach underground water. In times of severe drought, however, black rhinos will die from lack of water because they will not migrate.

◀ AFRICAN RHINOCEROSES STAY ON THE SAVANNA DURING DROUGHTS.

Rhino Paths
Are Ancient

Every day, rhinos travel over the same routes to watering holes and feeding areas. Their weight packs the soil into deep ruts, creating paths that are more than a foot deep. Many of these paths are ancient and have been shared by generations of rhinos.

Each rhino has its own home range, or territory. In dry seasons, rhinos will travel farther from their usual paths, but they will always remain in the boundaries of their home range.

[A group of rhinos is called a crash. A crash of rhinos usually consists of several pairs of mothers with their calves and the occasional adult male.]

▶ RHINOS STAY WITHIN THEIR HOME TERRITORIES.

Rhinos Need to Stay Cool

Rhinos live in hot, dry climates, as well as hot, humid ones. Rhinos do not have sweat glands, so they must cool down by drinking water, rolling in mud, and staying in the shade.

[Wallowing in a mud hole does more than keep a rhino cool. The mud dries on its skin, protecting it from sunburn and parasites.]

▼ MUD PROTECTS A RHINO'S SKIN FROM INSECTS AND SUNBURN.

▲ RHINOS SWIM TO KEEP COOL.

To avoid the midday heat, rhinos eat and search for food in the early morning or in the evening when the day is cooler. In the middle of the day, they find a shady place to rest, or they find a mud hole where they can wallow for a few hours. Indian rhinos live near rivers or swamps, where they can spend time swimming and wading.

Oxpeckers Help
Keep Rhinos Clean

Rhinos are hosts to a lot of parasites, such as ticks and fly larvae. Oxpeckers, or tickbirds, sit on the backs and faces of rhinos and pick the parasites from their backs, noses, and ears. Having fewer parasites makes rhinos healthier.

▼ OXPECKERS ARE ALSO KNOWN AS TICKBIRDS.

▲ BIRDS EAT INSECTS AND OTHER PARASITES FROM A RHINO'S BACK.

Oxpeckers are beneficial to rhinos in other ways, too. The birds have excellent eyesight, and they can see predators long before the rhino does. When an oxpecker sees a predator, it flies up in the air squawking. The rhino then prepares to run or attack. This type of relationship, in which two species benefit from each other, is called mutualism.

Rhino Bulls Will
Battle Each Other

A male rhino, or bull, is larger than the female. Sometimes, bulls challenge each other in tests of strength. If two rhinos are competing for a female, the fight can turn into a full-blown—and bloody—battle. Male rhinos are ready to mate at seven years of age, but they are not yet strong enough to engage in battles against older rhinos.

Rhino paths to watering holes are sprinkled with male urine. The scent helps mark the trail. Rhinos also spray urine at the borders of their territory to tell other rhinos to keep out. Male rhinos spray their urine every two or three minutes as they move around feeding.

[White rhinos are gentle and not easily angered. Black rhinos have a reputation for being the opposite, attacking for no apparent reason.]

▶ BULL RHINOS FIGHT OVER TERRITORY AND OVER FEMALES.

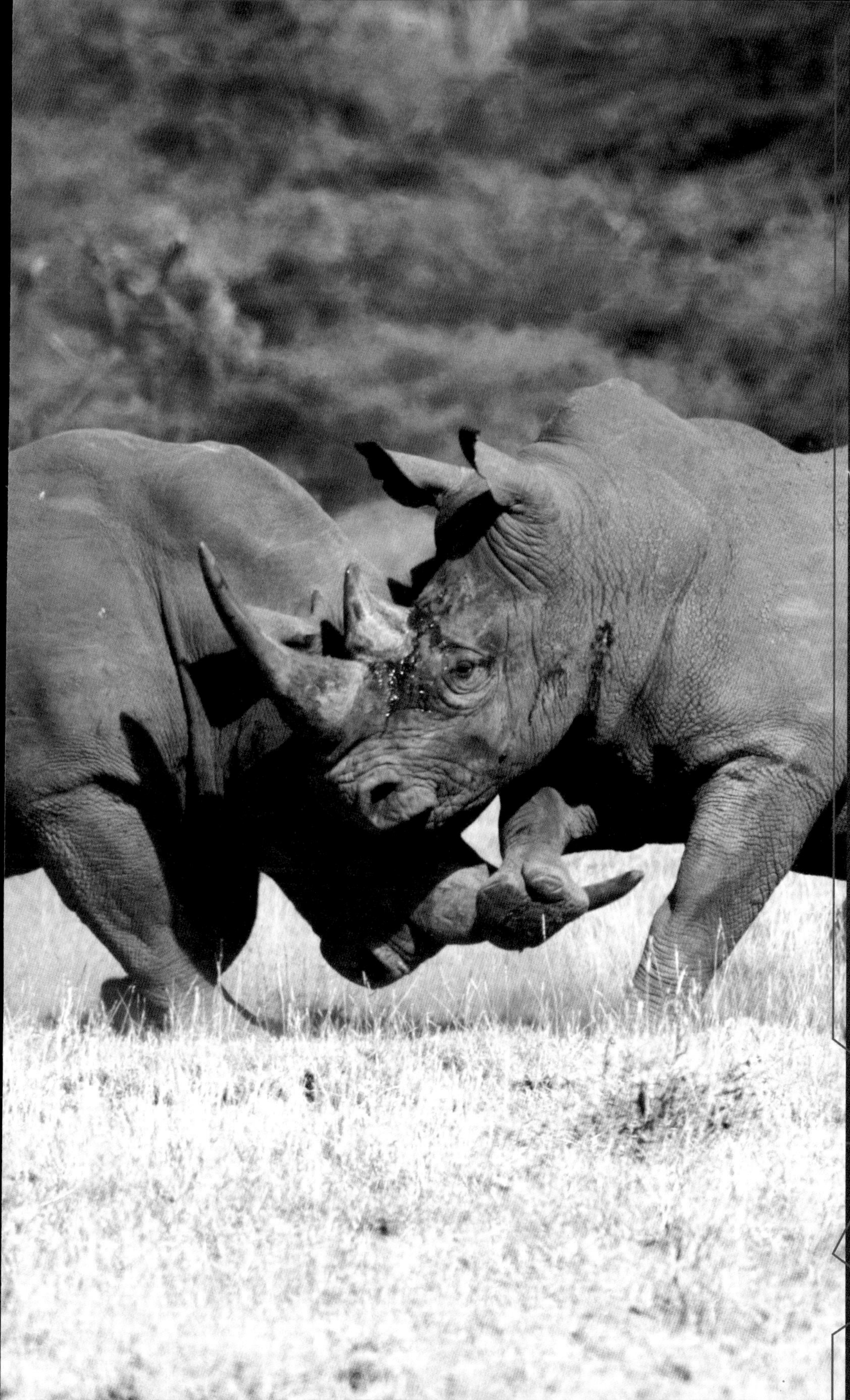

REASON TO CARE # 25
Female Rhinos Can Mate at Age Six

At around six years of age, female rhinos let the males know that they are ready to mate. They do this by whistling and spraying urine. When the male rhino, or bull, smells the scent, he begins his courtship. This is anything but gentle. The males and females roar and snort. They carry on this way for several days. Sometimes, the females even attack the males. Once the mating is complete, they go their separate ways.

[A male rhino is ready to mate when he is between the ages of seven and ten.]

◄ RHINOCEROS MATING CAN BECOME VIOLENT. THIS FEMALE (RIGHT) REJECTS THE MALE'S ADVANCES.

Mother Rhinos Protect Their Calves

A rhino's pregnancy lasts for fifteen or sixteen months. Researchers have found that just before a mother rhino gives birth, she grows more irritable and cranky than usual. When the time comes, she goes off alone and delivers her calf standing up. Mother rhinos are very protective of their newborns, and calves remain with their mothers for about three years.

▼ BLACK RHINOCEROS MOTHERS TEACH THEIR BABIES TO WALK BEHIND THEM.

▲ WHITE RHINOCEROS MOTHERS PROTECT THEIR CALVES FROM ATTACKS FROM BEHIND.

Black rhinos, which live mainly in forest and brush terrains, train their calves to walk behind them. Scientists believe this practice keeps predators at bay. Mother rhinos will see predators in the bushes before they can attack her calf. White rhinos, which travel in open savannas, do the opposite. These mothers make sure their calves stay in front of them, so no predators will surprise them from behind.

Rhino Calves
Are Born Big

White and Indian rhinos weigh between 100 and 150 pounds (45 and 70 kilograms) at birth. Newborn black rhinos weigh between 60 and 90 pounds (30 and 40 kilograms). Within hours of being born, a rhino baby is on its feet and nursing. The calf will nurse for at least a year, although it might start to eat small amounts of grass when it is three months old. A baby rhino can gain about 4 to 7 pounds a day on its mother's milk alone.

A newborn rhino does not have a horn. It has a firm, oval-shaped plate where its horn will later grow. When the baby is around one month old, a bump starts to form that is the beginning of a horn.

▶ THIS RHINO CALF HAS A BUMP WHERE ITS HORN IS BEGINNING TO GROW.

REASON TO CARE # 28

Rhinos Have Few Enemies

A predator in the wild will not interfere with a rhino, at least not for long. Other animals are no match for the large, powerful rhino. But baby rhinos, or calves, are more vulnerable. When a pack of lions or hyenas threatens a calf's safety, the rhino family group forms a circle around the calf. They stand with their deadly horns facing out. This lets predators know they had better look elsewhere for dinner.

The only real enemies of rhinos are humans, who destroy their habitats and poach them illegally for their horns.

◀ LIONS ARE USUALLY NO MATCH FOR AN ANGRY RHINOCEROS.

RHINOS IN CULTURE

REASON TO CARE # 29

Rhino Were Confused with Unicorns

The unicorn is a mythical animal. Today, it is imagined as a white horse with one long, spiraled horn. In ancient and medieval times, many people believed that the unicorn was a real animal. Confused travelers' descriptions of rhinos seem to have contributed to the unicorn myth.

When European explorer Marco Polo traveled through Asia around 1300, he described an animal he saw in Sumatra. His account clearly describes a Sumatran rhino, though Polo identified the animal as a unicorn. He wrote with disappointment that the unicorn was ugly and not at all how he had imagined it!

[Although the rhinoceros and the unicorn may not seem very alike, they have at least one legend in common. Myths about both creatures promise that their horns protect against poison.]

◄ THIS UNICORN STATUE SITS ABOVE A SCOTTISH CASTLE THAT WAS BUILT IN THE 1400s.

Rhino Horns Have Been Used as Medicine

It is a traditional practice in Asian medicine to grind rhinoceros horns into a powder, which is then used to treat nosebleeds, strokes, and fevers. There is no scientific proof that these traditional practices actually help.

From ancient times until the eighteenth or nineteenth century, people throughout Asia and Europe made rhino horn cups to detect poison. They believed that if a poisoned drink was poured into the cup, it would either foam up or be made harmless by the horn.

[Legends from Malaysia and Burma (also known as Myanmar) say that rhinos are natural firefighters. The animals will come out of the forest to stamp out a fire.]

▶ RHINOCEROS HORNS ARE USED IN TRADITIONAL MEDICINES.

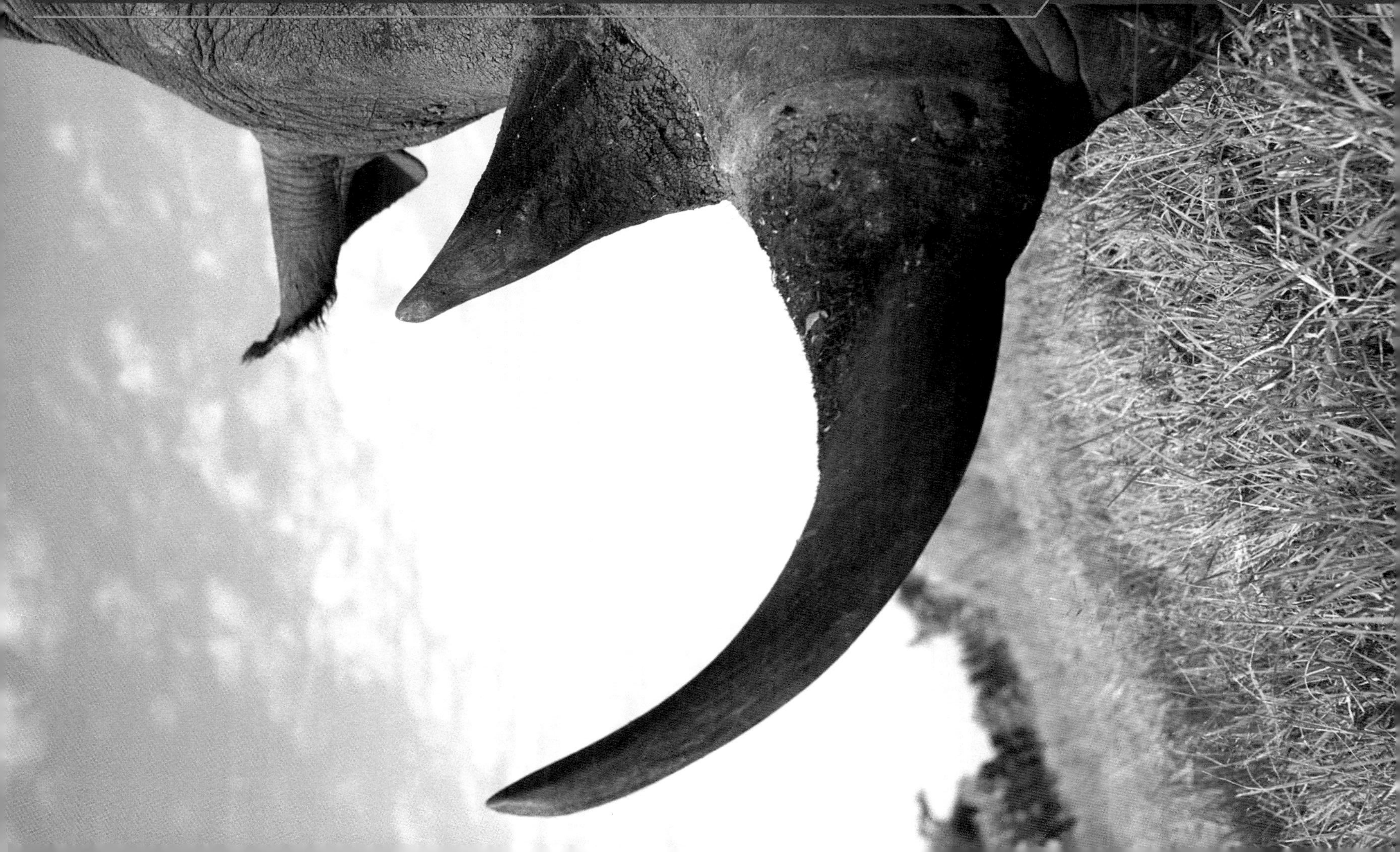

REASON TO CARE # 31

Rhino Horns Have Been Used for Ceremonies

For hundreds of years, the noblemen of Yemen in the Middle East have used rhino horns to make dagger handles. These ceremonial daggers are called *jambiyas*. Three tons of rhino horns were sold each year to Yemen during the 1970s. Since 1987, leaders in Yemen have enforced the ban on rhino horn trade. Yet, some are sold today illegally.

In ancient times, the people of China used rhino horns for ornamental and ceremonial purposes. Beginning in A.D. 600, they presented the emperor with a carved rhino horn cup on his birthday every year. These cups can be seen today in museums around the world. The Chinese also made buttons, combs, and paperweights from rhino horns.

[The Zulus of South Africa often carry a piece of rhino horn as a good luck charm.]

◄ IN YEMEN, MEN SELL DAGGERS MADE FROM RHINO HORNS.

Rhino Art
Raises Awareness

Asian rhinos at the Cincinnati Zoo are creating art to help rhinos in the wild. They are participating in a project called Rhino Rembrandts. Rembrandt was a famous Dutch painter. To create the art, zookeepers splash paint on canvases. The rhinos then use their lips to paint their creations. Visitors to the zoo can buy the rhinos' work, and the money is donated to conservation efforts.

Zookeeper Renee Carpenter helped start the program in 2005. She says, "It helps to keep [the rhinos'] minds sharp and helps to [re-create] some of the same behaviors they would experience in the wild."[1]

▶ SOME RHINOS ARE PAINTERS, SUCH AS THIS RHINO AT THE CINCINNATI ZOO WITH RENEE CARPENTER.

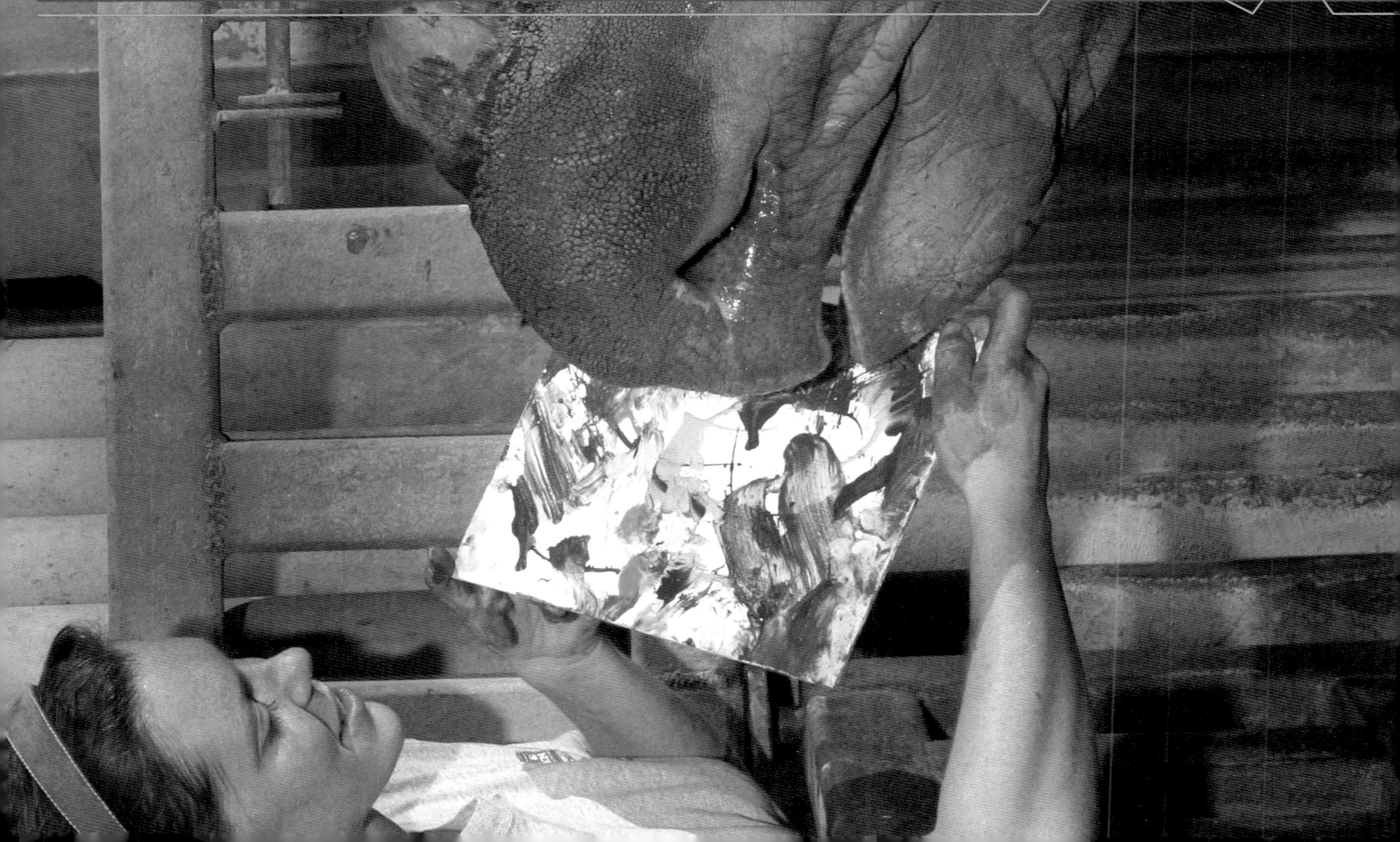

THREATS TO RHIINOS

REASON TO CARE # 33

Poaching Threatens Rhinos' Survival

The main cause of the rhino's decline in Asia and Africa is poaching. Rhinos are killed for their prized horns. A rhino horn is sold illegally for thousands of dollars, to be used for traditional medicines and other products.

Asian rhinos are the most threatened by poaching. Two Asian species, the Javan and the Sumatran, are critically endangered. There are only sixty Javan rhinos left in the wild, and none are in captivity. Only three hundred Sumatran rhinos are thought to be alive today, living in small areas in Sumatra, Borneo, and Malaysia.

◀ THIS CONTAINER WAS MADE FROM A POACHED RHINOCEROS FOOT.

Rhinos Are Losing Their Habitats

Another threat to rhinos' survival in Africa and Asia is loss of habitat. As the human population increases in Africa and Asia, more land is being taken over by homes and farms—land that used to be rhinos' habitat.

Loss of habitat leads to starvation in rhinos, because they rely on the forests, swamps, marshes, and grassy savannas for food.

[Climate change also contributes to habitat loss, as dry areas become even drier.]

► AS THEIR HABITATS SHRINK, RHINOCEROSES ARE COMING INTO CONFLICT WITH HUMANS.

REASON TO CARE # 35

African Rhino Populations Dropped Due to Poaching

Around one hundred and fifty years ago, more than 1 million rhinos roamed the forests and savannas of Africa. Then, hunting and habitat destruction by European settlers became an increasing problem. This was the main cause of enormous rhino losses in the late nineteenth and early twentieth centuries. Wealthy men from Europe and America also came to Africa on safari for the purpose of killing large game animals. They killed many rhinos for meat or for sport.

By the 1960s, hunting and poaching left only seventy thousand black rhinos and two thousand northern white rhinos remaining.

Demand for rhino horn increased during the 1970s and 1980s. Black rhino populations decreased by 96 percent during this time, and northern white rhino populations dropped from two thousand in 1960 to only fifteen in 1984.

[In the nineteenth century, Europeans used rhino horns for making whip handles, walking sticks, and door handles. They also used rhino horns to make handgrips on rifles and pistols. Panels on the insides of limousines were also made of rhino horns. These products have not been in demand, however, since the Great Depression during the 1920s and 1930s.]

◀ POACHING HAS LEFT RHINOS NEAR EXTINCTION IN AFRICA. THESE SKULLS ARE ALL FROM POACHED RHINOS.

Northern White Rhinos Have Been Wiped Out

The African white rhino is made up of two subspecies, the northern white and the southern white. Until recently, four northern white rhinos were alive in the protected Garamba National Park in the Democratic Republic of the Congo. However, in June 2008, TRAFFIC, a wildlife monitoring group, reported on its Web site that poachers had killed what might have been the last four northern white rhinos in the wild.

After one hundred years of protection, however, the southern white rhino is thriving. Fewer than one hundred southern white rhinos existed in the late nineteenth century. Due to conservation efforts during the last century, southern white rhinos are the only non-endangered rhinos in the world. They are considered near-threatened, an improved conservation status. There are around 17,500 southern white rhinos in Africa today. They live mainly in South Africa, with smaller populations in Botswana, Namibia, and Zimbabwe.

▶ THE NORTHERN WHITE RHINOCEROS IS NOW MOST LIKELY EXTINCT.

REASON TO CARE # 37

War Threatens Rhinos

During the Vietnam War in Southeast Asia in the 1960s and 1970s, a chemical weapon called Agent Orange defoliated forests. Defoliation, which makes leaves fall off plants, was a war strategy that made it harder for soldiers to hide in bushes and trees. Today, these forests have still not recovered. The scars of the war in Vietnam seriously impact rhinos, which can no longer return to their native habitat.

War and unstable governments are also a threat to African rhino populations. Private landowners in Zimbabwe created a safe haven for rhinos. But when people in Zimbabwe lost their land and homes in war, they claimed rhino habitat for their own. This has increased the risk of poaching because the land is no longer protected.

◄ U.S. AIRPLANES SPRAY DEFOLIATING CHEMICALS DURING THE VIETNAM WAR.

Rhinos Are in Conflict with Humans

Living near humans is a challenge for Asian rhinos. Vast areas of the rhinos' habitats have been destroyed due to human population growth. Rhinos are in conflict with people over the land that has not yet been developed. Rhinos have destroyed crops and have sometimes even killed people in these land conflicts. In other areas, land clearing for farms and buildings is the problem. Asian rhinos, which are totally dependent on their tropical forest habitat, face extinction unless humans intervene.

[When humans drain wetlands or clear forests in Asia, it ruins rhinoceros habitat.]

▶ MANY ASIAN RHINOCEROSES ARE LOSING THEIR HABITATS.

REASON TO CARE # 39

Inbreeding
Threatens Rhinos

Today, rhinos live in smaller territories than they did in the past because roads, buildings, and fences block their ability to wander. This also limits their choices during mating season, which leads to inbreeding. Inbreeding is mating between closely related individuals, and it can make rhinos more vulnerable to disease. Javan and Sumatran rhinos are at a high risk for inbreeding because there are so few individuals of each species left. To avoid the effects of inbreeding and to increase genetic diversity, conservation groups have begun moving rhinos to new locations.

[To avoid inbreeding, zoos use an online database to find mates from other zoos for their rare animals.]

◀ SUMATRAN RHINOCEROSES ARE AT RISK FOR INBREEDING BECAUSE THERE ARE FEW INDIVIDUALS LEFT.

REASON TO CARE # 40

Rhinos Are
Critically Endangered

Many animals in the wild are threatened by extinction. Rhinos and elephants, in particular, need protection from human behaviors, such as poaching and the wildlife trade.

Giving these animals a conservation status is a way to alert the public and to get community support to protect them. The International Union for the Conservation of Nature and Natural Resources (IUCN) is the world's authority on the conservation status of species. The organization created the IUCN Red List of Threatened Species in 1963. This list is made up of the conservation status of both plant and animal species. In 2008, the IUCN listed most types of rhinos as critically endangered. Only white rhinos and Indian rhinos are at a lower risk of extinction.

◄ BOTH RHINOCEROSES AND ELEPHANTS ARE ENDANGERED.

Breeding Rhinos
Helps Their Survival

The International Rhino Foundation supports Rhino Captive Programs. Even though the best place for rhinos is their natural habitat, rhinos in captivity may help the species survive.

[Zoos work hard to make sure a rhino's habitat looks like the real thing. Trees and mud holes are first on the list of items to include in the zoo habitat.]

The International Rhino Foundation's rhino advisory group manages rhino populations in zoos to ensure their survival. They make sure the rhinos have the best living conditions possible and are able to breed.

[A Sumatran rhino named Emi gave birth to a male baby rhino at the Cincinnati Zoo in 2001. It was the first Sumatran rhinoceros to be born in captivity.]

▶ RHINOCEROSES BORN IN ZOOS HELP KEEP THE SPECIES FROM BECOMING EXTINCT.

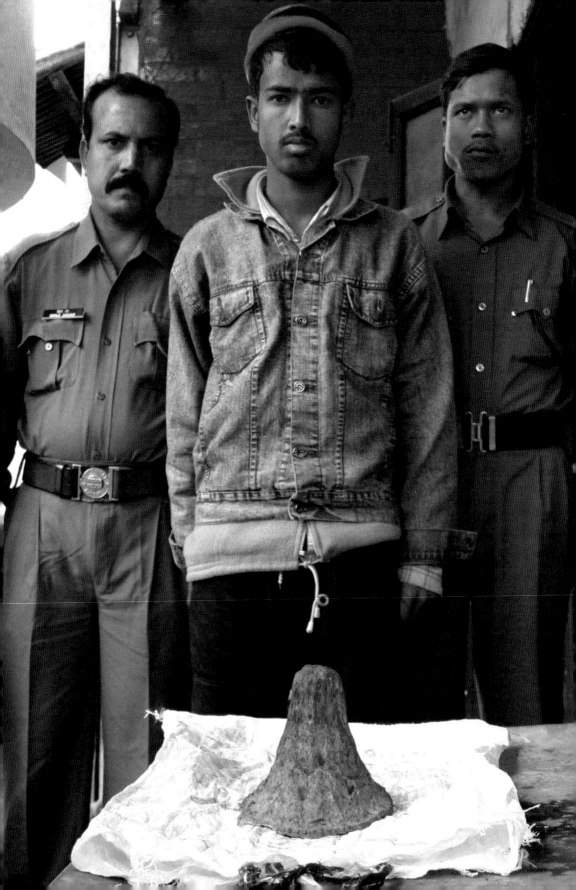

REASON TO CARE # 42

Laws Can Protect Rhinos

In Yemen, where rhino horns were once carved into dagger handles, there are new laws to protect rhinos. These laws have made it illegal for anyone to buy or to sell rhino horns. The daggers are now crafted using plastic or other materials. Many Chinese, who once used powdered rhino horn for medicine, are now using Western medicines instead, slowing demand for poachers.

Conservationists have worked hard to get similar laws passed in Africa. Their efforts have helped, because now poachers can be arrested. International law now bans the trade of rhino horns, which means people caught selling them can also be arrested.

In 1994, the United States declared that it would refuse to buy certain products from Taiwan, because Taiwan tolerated trade in rhino products. As a result, Taiwan stopped the trade.

◄ AN ACCUSED POACHER (CENTER) WAS CAUGHT WITH A RHINOCEROS HORN IN NORTHERN INDIA.

Local Groups Can Protect Rhinos from Poachers

SOS Rhino is an international foundation dedicated to preserving the five rhino species. In Malaysia, SOS Rhino trains groups of boys to be members of Rhino Protection Units. They watch over and protect rhinos from poachers.

The boys come from local hunting communities and already know the jungle very well. They are trained to take photographs, take samples, drive motorboats, read maps, and understand rhino behavior.

▼ ANTI-POACHING PATROLS PROTECT LOCAL RHINOS.

▲ GAME WARDENS RIDING AN ELEPHANT PATROL FOR POACHERS.

[The intense efforts of SOS Rhino in Malaysia have decreased Sumatran rhino poaching and habitat loss. However, the organization must prevent rhino inbreeding in order to save the species from extinction.]

REASON TO CARE # 44

Poachers Still Kill Rhinos Without Horns

In 1992, government officials in Zimbabwe shot tranquilizer darts into every rhino they could find. Then, they safely cut off each rhino's horn, leaving only a short stump. Officials believed that poachers would leave the rhinos alone if their horns were removed. But poachers still killed the rhinos for the remaining stump. Also, removing the rhinos' horns made it harder for the animals to protect themselves. This failed approach to rhino conservation caused a sharp decline in Africa's black rhino population during the 1990s.

[The World Wildlife Fund (WWF) supports a sanctuary program in Kenya where rhinos are kept in fenced areas. Rhino populations are moved between sanctuaries to make sure the species does not become inbred.]

◀ REMOVING A RHINO'S HORN WILL NOT STOP POACHERS FROM KILLING IT.

People Can Stop the Illegal Wildlife Trade

TRAFFIC is a group that monitors the wildlife trade. They raise awareness about poaching and make sure that trade in wild plants and animals, such as rhinos, is not a threat to a species' conservation. In 1998, after TRAFFIC reported that medicines in Canada and the United States included tiger and rhinoceros ingredients, the United States Congress passed the Rhino and Tiger Product Labeling Act. This made it illegal in the United States to import or export anything labeled as having ingredients from tigers or rhinos.

The Convention on International Trade in Endangered Species (CITES) is an agreement between nations around the world. It states that governments will not endanger the survival of a species by trading wild animals and plant life. TRAFFIC provides information and assistance to CITES on a regular basis. Together, they form a team approach to conservation.

▶ TRAFFIC AND CITES WORK TO PROTECT RHINOCEROSES SUCH AS THIS INDIAN RHINO.

REASON TO CARE # 46

Scientists Can Track Rhinos by Their Footprints

Scientists have learned that fitting rhinos with tracking devices (such as radio collars, ear notches, and horn implants) creates problems. These devices create stress for the animals and cause female rhinos to become less fertile.

To keep track of rhinos and to better serve the scientists' needs, researchers have developed a new plan. They take digital photographs of rhino footprints. Each rhino's footprints are unique, which makes it possible to track individual rhinos by using these images. This method is beginning to replace tranquilizing in some situations.

◀ THESE MEN HAVE TRANQUILIZED THIS RHINO IN ORDER TO FIT IT WITH A RADIO COLLAR.

Groups Can Work Together to Protect Rhinos

Conservationists recognized that if rhinos and elephants were going to survive, law-enforcement agencies, governments, and local communities would have to work together toward the animals' protection. The World Wildlife Fund (WWF) agreed and created the Asian Rhino and Elephant Action Strategy. Its goals are to save habitats from destruction and enforce laws against poaching. The Action Strategy strives to help humans and rhinos (as well as other animals) share the land. It teaches people who live near important habitats how to use their land in sustainable ways—preserving their livelihoods while preserving the environment.

▶ THE ASIAN RHINO AND ELEPHANT ACTION STRATEGY HELPS HUMANS AND ANIMALS SHARE THE LAND.

REASON TO CARE # 48

Rhinos Need
Space to Roam

The South African province of KwaZulu-Natal is home to many of African's 3,725 endangered black rhinos. The area's conservation group is working with local landowners, whose property was once the home of black rhinos. The landowners have joined together and agreed to remove their fences so rhinos may roam freely again through these habitats.

A World Wildlife Fund (WWF) survey found the largest known Sumatran rhino population in the heart of Borneo—thirteen animals in 2005. WWF is working with local groups to monitor the animals and to prevent poaching. They are also working with landowners and governments to prevent losing local forests to palm oil and timber plantations. They say the destruction of those forests will eventually lead to poaching of the remaining Sumatran rhinos.

◀ THIS ELECTRIC FENCE IN KENYA PROTECTS BLACK RHINOS BY KEEPING THEM SEPARATE FROM PEOPLE.

Rhinos Depend
on Humans

Rhinos, the fearless beasts of the wild, are now dependent on humans for survival. Poaching has slowed down because of laws against it, but it is still a serious problem. Sadly, the safest place for rhinos is in one of the many sanctuaries where electric fences and steady patrols keep poachers away. The American Zoo Association's Species Survival Plan has breeding programs that make sure rhino species survive in captivity. Some rhino populations are growing in the wild, but most are still declining.

▶ THIS SUMATRAN RHINO IS PROTECTED IN A SANCUTARY.

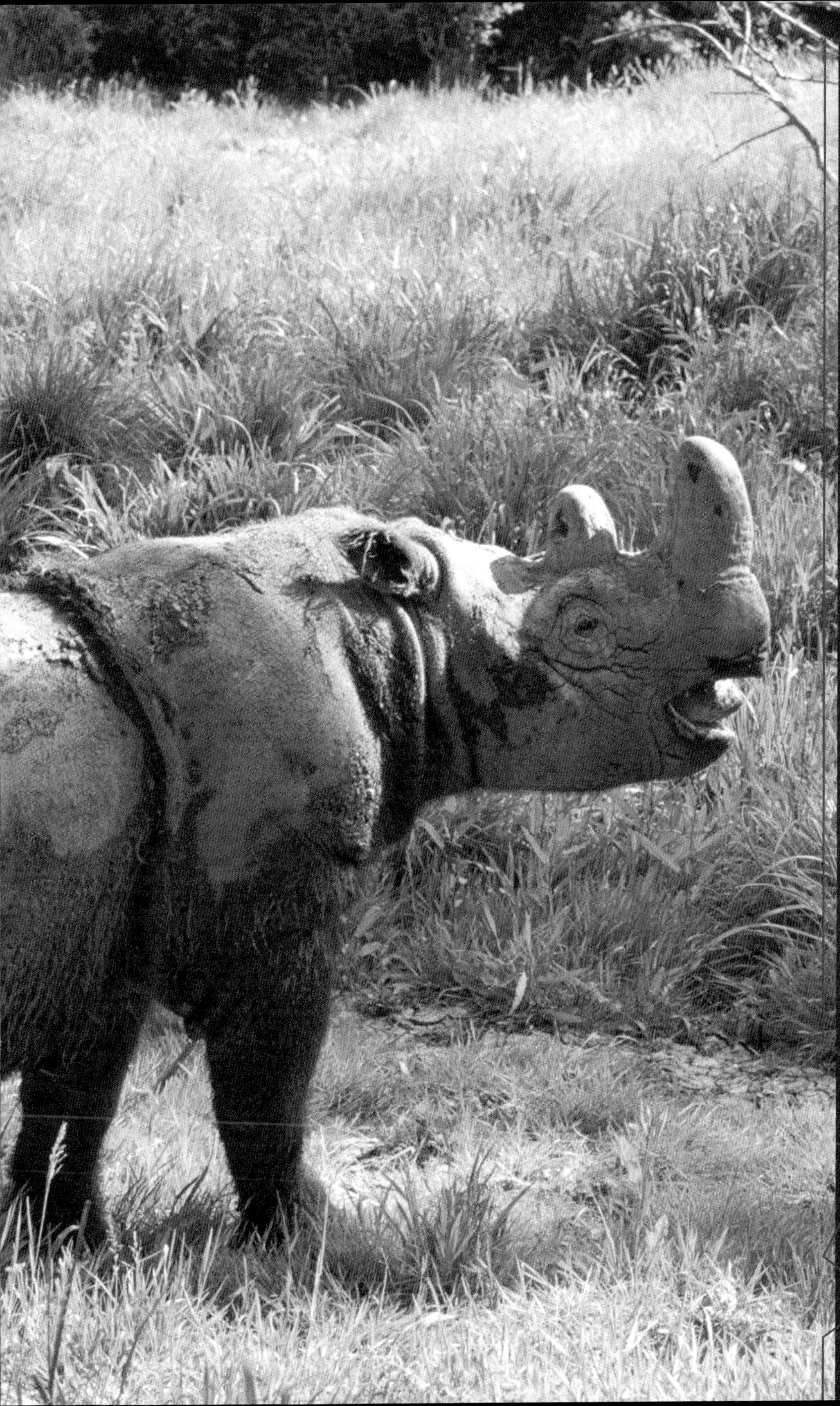

You Can Help Save Rhinos

Fun and Rewarding Ways to Help Save Rhinos

- Read books and articles to learn more about rhinos.
- Visit zoos to see rhinos up close.
- Keep informed. Read the WWF's and other conservation groups' Web sites for updates about rhino populations.
- If you travel to places where rhino products are sold, fight the illegal wildlife trade by not buying these products.
- When buying wood products, check for the Forest Stewardship Council or Sustainable Forestry Initiative label. These labels let you know you are supporting responsible forest management.
- Recycling helps protect trees. Participate in your community's recycling program.
- Write an article about rhinos or conservation for your student newspaper.
- Have your class plan a fund-raiser to support rhino conservation.

▶ YOU CAN HELP SAVE RHINOS!

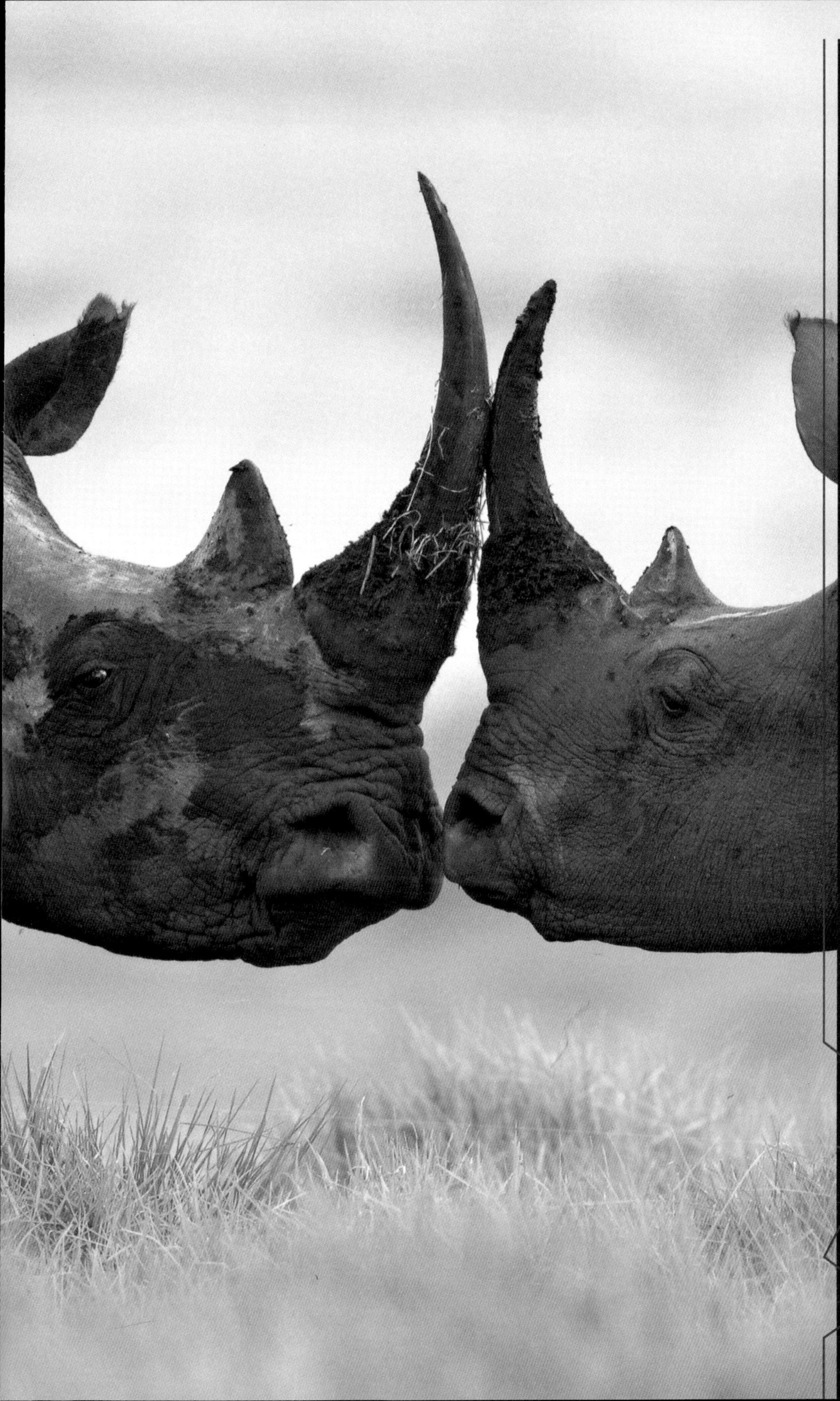

GLOSSARY

captivity—Being in a zoo instead of the wild.

conservation—The protection of nature and animals.

diversity—Variety.

drought—A period of time in which there is not enough water or rain.

endangered—At risk of becoming extinct.

environment—The natural world; the area in which a person or animal lives.

extinct—Died out completely.

habitat—The place in which an animal lives; the features of that place including plants, landforms, and weather.

herbivore—An animal that eats only plants.

inbreeding—Mating between two individuals that are too closely related.

incisor—A tooth at the front of the mouth that is used for cutting.

infrasound—Low sounds, below human ability to hear.

mammal—A warm-blooded animal with hair; female mammals nurse their young.

molar—A tooth located in the back of the mouth used for grinding food.

order—A category of similar families, or groups, of animals.

parasite—An organism that lives on a plant or animal of another species and benefits from that host.

poach—To illegally kill or steal protected wild animals.

population—The total number of a group of animals.

prehensile—Able to grab or take hold of something.

prehistoric—From a time before written history.

range—The entire area in which a species lives; the territory of an individual animal or group of animals.

sanctuary—An area of land that is safe from hunters.

savanna—A grassland with scattered trees and shrubs.

species—A specific group of animals with shared physical characteristics and genes; members within a species can breed with each other to produce offspring.

subspecies—A group within a species that is different from other groups in that species.

temperate—Moderate, not too hot or too cold.

territory—An area defended by one animal against others.

FURTHER READING

Books

Hamilton, Garry. *Rhino Rescue*. Richmond Hill, ON: Firefly Books, 2006.

McGavin, George. *Endangered: Wildlife on the Brink of Extinction*. Richmond Hill, ON: Firefly Books, 2006.

Thomas, Isabel. *Elephant vs. Rhinoceros*. Chicago, IL: Raintree, 2006.

Toon, Ann, and Steve Toon. *Rhinos: Worldlife Library Series*. Stillwater, WI: Voyageur Press, 2002.

Internet Addresses

National Geographic Kids: Black Rhinoceroses
<http://kids.nationalgeographic.com/Animals/CreatureFeature/Black-rhinoceros>

World Wildlife Fund: About African Rhinos
<http://www.panda.org/what_we_do/endangered_species/endangered_species_list/rhinoceros/african_rhinos/>

World Wildlife Fund: About Asian Rhinos
<http://www.panda.org/what_we_do/endangered_species/endangered_species_list/rhinoceros/asian_rhinos/>

SOURCE NOTES

Source Notes

1. Gail Towns, "Painting for a Purpose," *AroundCinci.com*, March 10, 2006, <http://www.aroundcinci.com/gen_includes/article.asp?articleid=3842> (July 17, 2008).

INDEX